Inside Machines
Fire Engines
and Other Rescue Vehicles

David West

WINDMILL
BOOKS ™

Published in 2018 by **Windmill Books**,
an imprint of Rosen Publishing
29 East 21st Street, New York, NY 10010

Designed and illustrated David West

Cataloging-in-Publication Data
Names: West, David.
Title: Fire Engines and other rescue vehicles / David West.
Description: New York : Windmill Books, 2018. | Series: Inside machines | Includes index.
Identifiers: ISBN 9781499483307 (pbk.) | ISBN 9781499483246 (library bound) | ISBN 9781499483123 (6 pack)
Subjects: LCSH: Fire engines–Juvenile literature. | Emergency vehicles–Juvenile literature.
Classification: LCC TH9372.W47 2018 | DDC 629.225–dc23

Manufactured in the United States of America

CPSIA Compliance Information: Batch BS17WM: For Further Information contact Rosen Publishing, New York, New York at 1-800-237-9932

Contents

Ambulance

Modern ambulances are like hospitals on wheels. They carry lifesaving equipment, such as **defibrillators** to restart a person's heart. They rush to the scene of an emergency at high speed with lights flashing and **sirens** wailing. After the patient has been cared for the ambulance takes them to a hospital.

*A **paramedic** on a bicycle has arrived before the ambulance. An injured skateboarder is stretchered into the ambulance.*

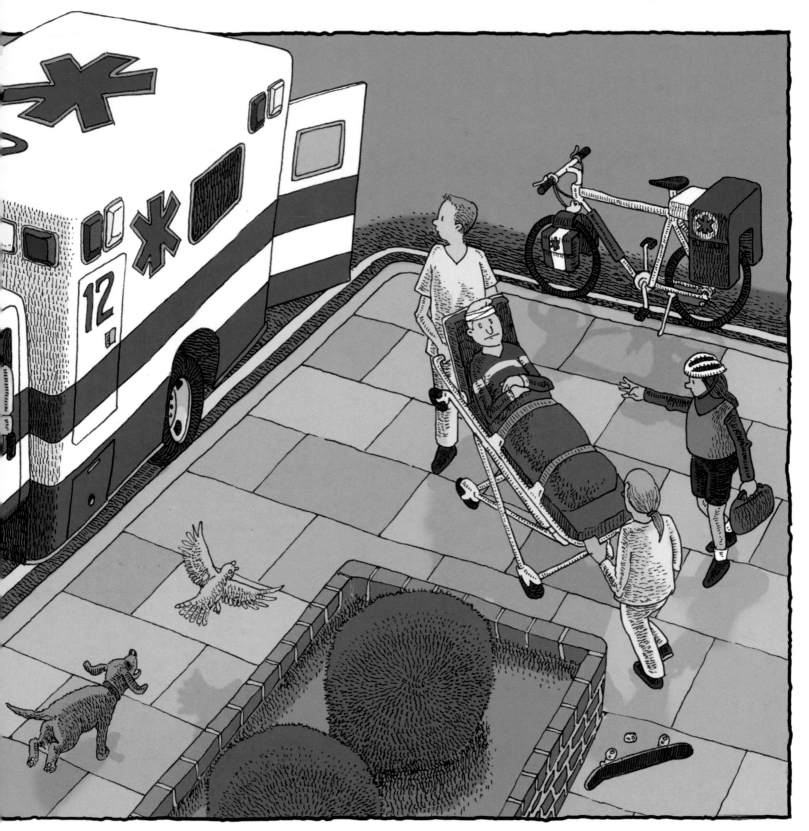

Electrical equipment
Medical lifesaving equipment includes heart monitors.

Oxygen
Portable oxygen cylinder and mask

Stretcher
This has wheels with a folding base to fit inside the ambulance.

Storage
There is plenty of room for medicine, blankets, and equipment.

Light

Paramedic
There are two paramedics. One travels in the back with the patient.

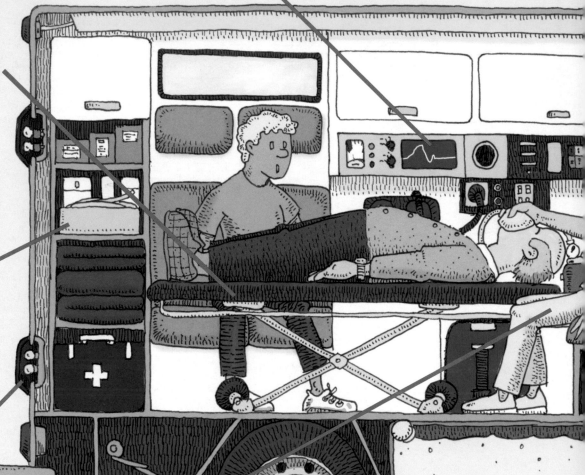

Inside an **Ambulance**

Oxygen cylinder
A large cylinder provides oxygen for the patients while they are being taken to the hospital.

Radio unit
The driver receives messages on the radio and can speak to the hospital about the patient before they arrive.

Engine

Batteries
These supply power to the electrical equipment as well as to the engine.

Driver
The driver is also a trained paramedic.

Fire engine

When a fire breaks out, fire engines race to the building on fire. Long ladders are used to rescue people from tall buildings and to spray water from hoses. Firefighters wear special clothing and have oxygen tanks to protect them when they enter a blazing building.

A long ladder with a hose is attached to a turntable. A firefighter directs the water jet from the turntable.

Inside a **Fire engine**

Hoses
200-foot-long (61 m) hoses are rolled and stored here.

Crew
There are five crew members including the driver.

Driver

Engine

Siren
Along with flashing lights, the sound of the siren warns other vehicles to keep clear.

Pump controls
Water is pumped from the water tank or a nearby fire hydrant.

Ladder

The ladder can extend to reach windows at the top of a building so that people can be rescued.

Turntable

This uses gears to turn the ladder and moves it up or down with a hydraulic ram.

Hydraulic ram

Steps

Water tank

A fire engine can carry about 1,000 gallons (3,785 L) of water.

Equipment

Rescue tools and breathing equipment are stored in lockers at the side.

Lifeboat

Lifeboats are designed to speed to the rescue of people in danger at sea. They are built to withstand violent seas in stormy weather. If they capsize, they turn the right way up immediately. They are kept in special stations around the coast. The crews are highly trained and most are unpaid volunteers.

Inside a **Lifeboat**

Crew

There are six crew members including the coxswain.

Radar and aerial mast

Inflatable life rafts

In the unlikely event the lifeboat sinks, the crew uses the life rafts.

Life ring

These are thrown to people in the water to help them stay afloat until they are rescued.

Exhaust

Engine

The lifeboat is powered by two large diesel engines.

Propeller

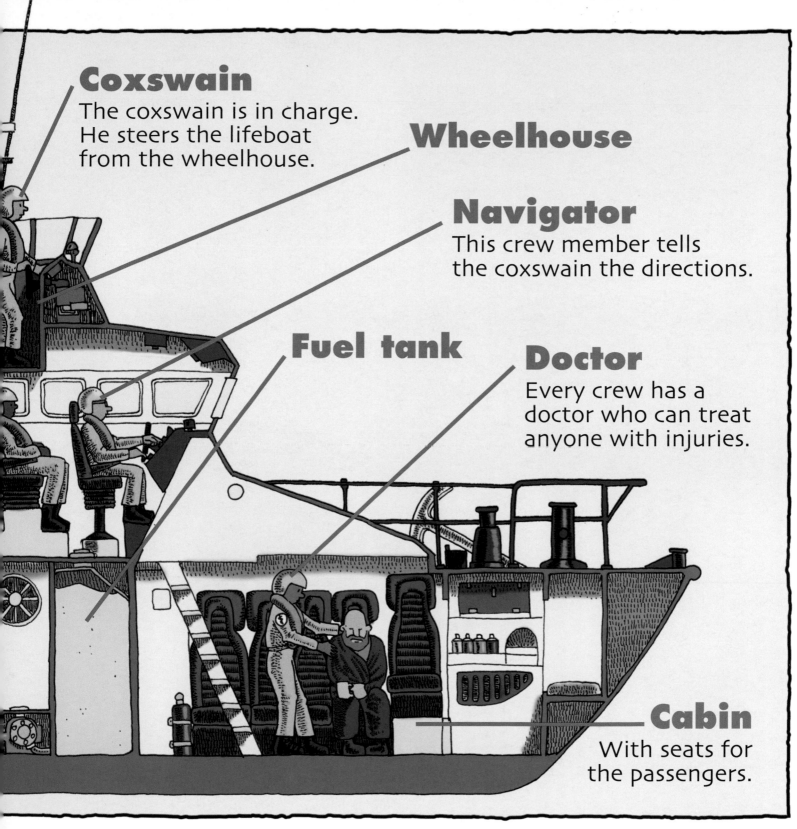

Coxswain
The coxswain is in charge. He steers the lifeboat from the wheelhouse.

Wheelhouse

Navigator
This crew member tells the coxswain the directions.

Fuel tank

Doctor
Every crew has a doctor who can treat anyone with injuries.

Cabin
With seats for the passengers.

Police car

Police cars are fast and powerful. They are used by police departments in most countries. Some are used as patrol cars. They cruise neighborhoods, ready to speed to an incident and rescue people in danger. Others are used as pursuit cars to catch criminals in high-speed car chases.

Police cars like this one are sometimes called "black and whites," because they are painted in these colors.

Flashing lights

In emergencies, police cars use flashing lights and sirens to warn other drivers to let them pass.

Grill

A wire mesh grill separates the back from the front.

Suspect

People suspected of committing a crime are put in the back seat.

Spare tire

Fuel tank

Shotgun

In addition to a handgun, police officers have other weapons, such as shotguns, in the car.

Inside a Police car

Spotlight
A movable light helps police officers spot criminals in the dark.

Computer
A laptop computer sits on the passenger seat. It is linked to police databases and can help in many ways, from identifying criminals to **gps** navigation.

Exhaust

Engine
Police cars have powerful engines that are ideal for high-speed car chases.

A Sikorsky Coast Guard helicopter uses its winch to lift an injured sailor to safety.

COAST GUARD

HOUSTON

Rescue helicopter

Search and rescue helicopters can reach people in trouble at sea quicker than lifeboats. They can travel at 155 mph (249 km). A winchman is lowered down to the deck of a ship or even into the sea to pick up injured or drowning people. Once on board the helicopter, the injured are given first aid and flown to the hospital.

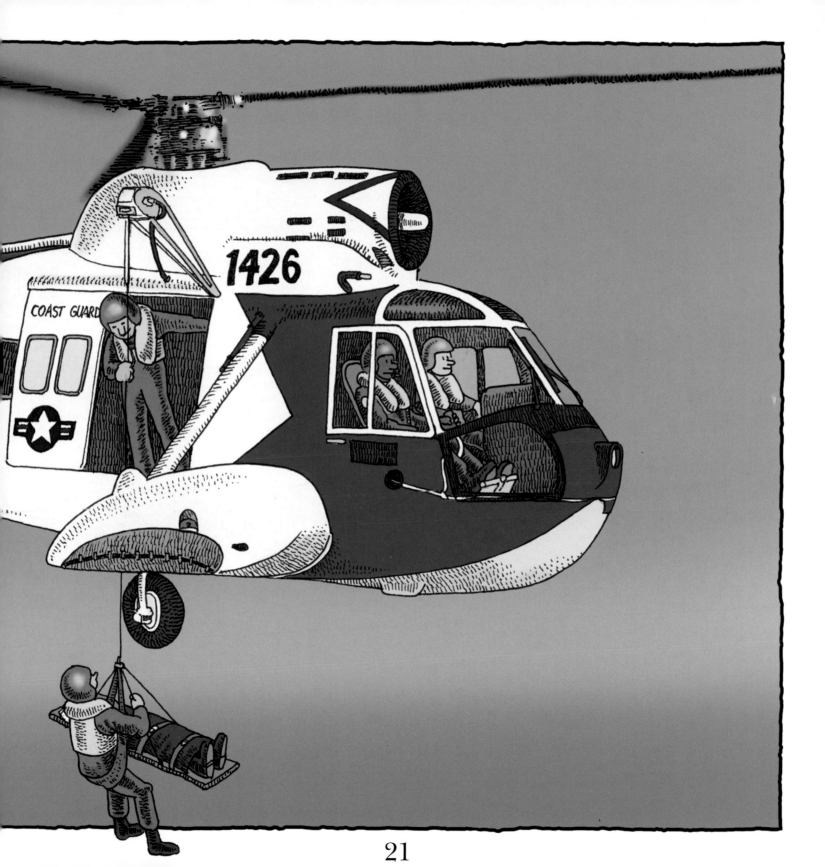

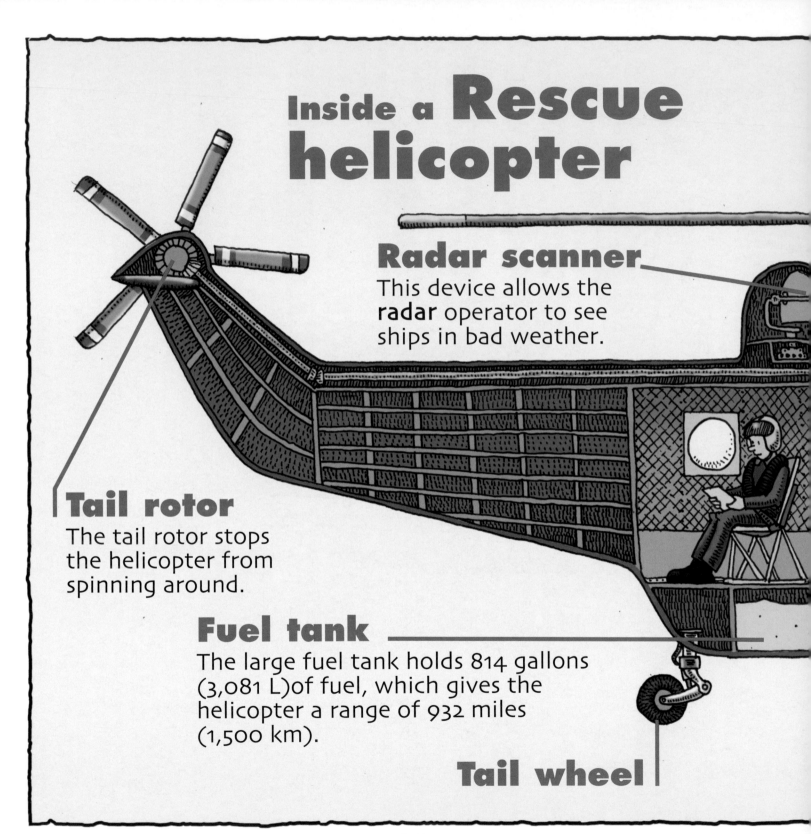

Inside a **Rescue helicopter**

Radar scanner

This device allows the **radar** operator to see ships in bad weather.

Tail rotor

The tail rotor stops the helicopter from spinning around.

Fuel tank

The large fuel tank holds 814 gallons (3,081 L)of fuel, which gives the helicopter a range of 932 miles (1,500 km).

Tail wheel

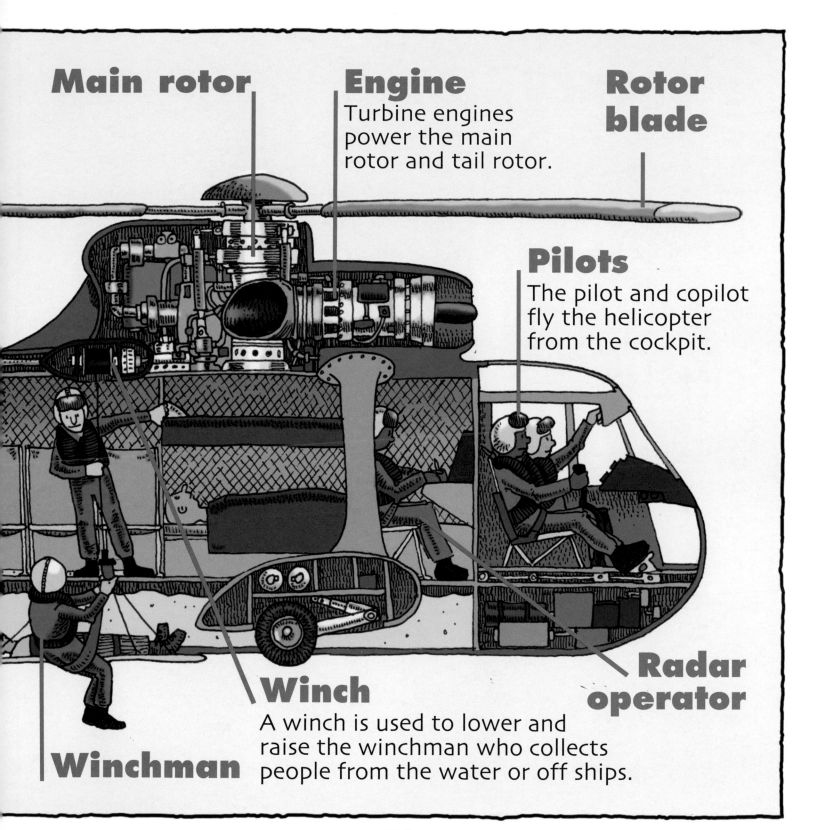

Main rotor

Engine
Turbine engines power the main rotor and tail rotor.

Rotor blade

Pilots
The pilot and copilot fly the helicopter from the cockpit.

Winch
A winch is used to lower and raise the winchman who collects people from the water or off ships.

Radar operator

Winchman

Glossary

defibrillator
An electrical device that restarts the heart.

gps (global positioning system)
A way of finding your position using signals from satellites.

paramedic
A medical professional trained to respond to emergency calls.

radar
A system that detects objects using radio waves and displays their position on a screen.

siren
A device that makes a loud, wailing, warning sound.

Index